THE
Archive Photographs
SERIES

TEIGNMOUTH

Wishing you a happy Christmas.

Photo by Denney.   Teignmouth.

DEVON COUNTY TEIGNMOUTH

THE
Archive Photographs
SERIES

TEIGNMOUTH

Compiled by
Viv Wilson

CHALFORD

First published 1997
Copyright © Viv Wilson, 1997

The Chalford Publishing Company
St Mary's Mill, Chalford,
Stroud, Gloucestershire, GL6 8NX

ISBN 0 7524 0761 9

Typesetting and origination by
The Chalford Publishing Company
Printed in Great Britain by
Bailey Print, Dursley, Gloucestershire

*To all those who hold Teignmouth close to their heart,
in particular the people who have helped make this volume a reality.*

Contents

Acknowledgements

Buddy Bearne, Mrs P. Ball, Harold Bucklow, Bob and Wyn Barge, Harold and Wendy Banwell, Ken and Win Bennett, Margaret Bircham, Betty Blake, Jim and Eva Breed, Anthony and Elizabeth Brenner, Ken Boobyer, Ernie Chapman, Gerry Chapman, Mary Collins, Dennis Cook, Elizabeth Currie, Ted Collins, The late Mable Coleridge, Flo Darke, Neta Drew, Alf and Kathleen Dodd, Brian Dodd, Joyce East, Brian Estill (Curator of Devon and Cornwall Constabulary Museum), Rita Furler, David and Liz Golder, Eileen Gray, Grace Griffiths, Mrs Gibbons, Syd and Mavis Hook, Phyllis Hook, Wesley Highgate, Tom Highgate, Julie Hill, Ken Holmes, P. Hooper, Shirley and Colin Ingram, Beryl Jones, Cynthia and Peter Lewis, Steve Leyman, May Loveridge, June and Len Matthews, Audrey and Reg Matthews, Peggy and Robin Mole, Rita and Ernest Menghini, Noreen Mardon, Fred Medland, Peter and the late Gwen Mole, The late Warren Miles, The late Noel Nathan, Pat and Albert Penwill, Dorcas Porter, Pat and Peter Prince, Harold Pedrick, Jane Northcott, Margaret Quantick, John and Jill Reed, Vicky Rose, Pauline Rossi, Christine and Harry Sealey, Eric Searle, Pauline Seaton, John Silverman, Arthur Smith, Joan Squire, Glenda Steer, Nell and Bill Tibbs, Fred Tooley, Gordon and the late Maudie Tosio, Mrs Trankle, Teignmouth Museum and Historical Society, Teignmouth Town Council. Margaret Upchurch, Paul Warner, Edith Wareham, the late Gordon Walker, Margaret Whitlock, Nicky Whitlock, Angela and John Ward, David Weekes, Freda Welton, Margaret Wood, Marina Webb and Margaret Yandell.

Bibliography

History of Teignmouth by Grace Griffiths
Exeter-Newton Abbot. A Railway History by Peter Kay
Teignmouth - a Maritime History by H.J. Trump
Visitor's Guide to Teignmouth by Ann Pearson
From Teignmouth with love by Viv Wilson
Teignmouth in old picture postcards, volume 2 by Viv Wilson

Introduction

Dates become particularly significant when a new century is but two years ahead. Interest in nostalgia attains new heights - almost as if we doubt our ability to carry memories across the millennium threshold. Photographic collections such as this become a subscription to posterity acting as 'aide-memoires' for those with long-term recall, and a book of revelations to newcomers.

The earliest images in the following pages date from about 1870. By the time the first cumbersome plate cameras began to record its features, Teignmouth had acquired over a thousand years of diverse chronicles. It developed from a small settlement of fisher folk and salt makers in 800 AD to an international port and favoured south coast resort by the end of the Victorian epoch.

On two occasions, Teignmouth was almost eradicated. The French invasion of 1690 left two hundred and forty inhabitants homeless. In the Second World War, two hundred and twenty-eight houses were lost in twenty-one air raids. Both incursions resulted in major re-development some arguably inappropriate. Teignmouth endeavours to take progress in her stride, rewarding the violators of her beauteous features with a gracious smile.

Saunter through the following pages and ponder encapsulated moments of yesteryear. Reflect upon lost features and others that have replaced them. Study the faces of those who helped make Teignmouth what it was. Above all, enjoy!

Viv Wilson
September 1997

East Beach from Jubilee Shelter, *c.* 1938.

One
The Heart of Town

The journey into the past begins.................

The Triangle at the beginning of the twentieth century.

The trio of top hat wearers hover, determined to be included in the scene. The building with distinctive turrets marking the end of Wellington Street was relatively new and on the adjacent corner, beneath the oak (planted in 1837 when Victoria became queen) was a retailer of footwear.

Mates's Illustrated Directory of 1906 provides a record of two Triangle businesses. F.E. Vick, bootmaker, retailed 'Queen' label footwear. By the 1930s the shop had become Lennards where it was possible to purchase shoes and bags made of crocodile and alligator skin.

The Royal Library offered a reading room free to subscribers. W.H. Day sold view maps and guide books and catered for photographers by offering a range of materials as well as use of a darkroom. The roof ornamentations appear to represent a lion and unicorn set up with a flagpole. The ogee windows of the upper floor have survived at least to the time of writing.

The famous chain of stationers have occupied the Royal Library from the 1920s. Teign Cars charabanc trips to Widecombe and Becky Falls are advertised on blackboards (left) and despite poor roads and bone-shaking travel, there was no shortage of takers. Note the folding canvas hood at the rear of the vehicle.

The Triangle in the early 1920s. A crowd has gathered to mark the presentation of a stone urn to the people of Teignmouth from numerous Belgian refugees from the Great War. The geranium-filled urn placed on a rockery mound, was later removed to French Street. In recent years, the urn has been moved once more (minus the mound) to a flower bed adjacent to the Den bowling green. The original plate was exposed from a window of No.2 The Triangle once occupied by Hindley Photographers. The plate together with numerous negatives was discovered on the premises by later occupants. Although it had been cracked, the resultant print is a wonderfully detailed record. The fountain next to the oak is something of a puzzle for it appears to be draped with material or flags rather than water cascades. To the rear of the cab driver's shelter, the gas lamp bears a small finger post indicating an enquiry bureau in the area of Station Road. People not wearing hats in those times were considered to be improperly dressed - the ladies millinery confections bringing a sense of 'occasion' to the event. Whilst most of the male onlookers wear boaters, caps or trilby hats, the dignitaries have respectfully removed their headgear whilst the learned-looking gentleman with the fulsome white beard addresses the crowd.

VE Day, 9 May 1945. Wellington Street bedecked with celebratory bunting. It was recorded that the spirit of Teignmouth's people was never beaten and no praise was too high of their stoicism and the performance of its civil defence and utility services personnel - two of whom gained recognition from King George VI. A BEM was granted to J.S. Scown and Brigadier General J. Morrison received an MBE.

The winter of 1947 brought Arctic conditions - the worst weather recorded since the late nineteenth century. There is no sign of the Triangle's garden plot, progress demanded the construction of public conveniences (left) in the 1920s. Local bus stops were established on each of the three sides and that is how it remained for about seventy years.

A scheme costing £600,000 transformed the Triangle into a pedestrian priority zone in 1995. Indignation at the removal of the public conveniences coupled with disappointment in the stark slabs and lack of floral features caused much comment in the local press. It was dubbed 'Red Square' by some!

Restoration of the Wills fountain, March 1995.

John Scown (right) and Arthur Full next to the Wills fountain originally erected on the Esplanade in 1885 but moved to Little Triangle in the 1920s.

Ponies and elephants from a visiting circus use the fountain as a watering hole in the 1930s. An outbreak of diphtheria caused the council to cut off the water supply until some sixty years later when it was restored to provide a focal point for the enhancement of the Triangles.

A police constable on duty in Den Road in the early twentieth century.

Wellington Street from Bank Street in the early twentieth century. Rossiter's the jeweller and goldsmith occupied the corner site (right) and the drum clock thoughtfully provided by Mr Rossiter in 1909 is just visible. A carrier has paused with his handcart, a non-polluting if tedious conveyance for delivery of goods to local businesses.

Tucked in behind Station Road, Devonshire Place was parallel to Bickford Lane joining Lower Brook Street with the boundary of Brook Hill Infant and Junior School. Early in the 1970s, work began on the demolition of the Place, school and adjacent properties in order to create a car park. In 1997 despite considerable local opposition, the construction of a new supermarket on this site caused another huge upheaval for the town.

Regent Street in the 1940s. The town's trade was characteristically generated through numerous individual shops that in earlier times included basket makers, hatters, blacksmiths and watchmakers. Regent Street had a chemist shop, milk bar, a pair of cafes and a hairdressing parlour. The double-deck bus from Exeter is approaching the Triangle bus stops, having descended Dawlish Hill.

The junction of Dawlish Street with Regent Street in the early twentieth century. The fine tower of St Michael's church standing sentinel over the eastern end of town was built in 1887 to commemorate Queen Victoria's Golden Jubilee. Vehicles approaching from Dawlish had to negotiate the narrow corner.

Before major alterations to the through traffic system, vehicles descending Dawlish Road needed good brakes - something this timber lorry lacked in the 1930s when it failed to negotiate the bend and crashed into the Dawlish Inn (Dicey O'Reilly's from 1996)

As traffic increased, a post-war measure to assist motorists 'see' around the blind corner was a convex mirror positioned outside the Dawlish Inn. Local coach driver, Bill Brown holds the small child high for his daughter Pat to take the picture.

Station Road lost several buildings during re-development in the 1970s. One was the Police Station pictured in 1911 with decorations marking the coronation of King George V and Queen Mary.

The Star Restaurant was attached to Partridge's Hotel currently Roundel Club. Next to that was Hayman's Monumental Mason's Works. *Catherine the Great* was showing at the Riviera Cinema according to the notice board left of the door sometime around 1928.

On the opposite side of the road stood the Railway Hotel. Note the gateposts at either side of the entrance to Station Yard then, in your imagination, turn left out of the picture, into Brook Street East and continue along to the corner.

This picture from the 1970s follows on from the last - note the gatepost at Station Yard once more, it is almost as tall as the telephone box. The red, multi-paned boxes fell from favour in the 1980s and were replaced by bland but hygienic public pay phones. The Sebastopol Inn was one of over thirty hostelries in the town. Salisbury Villa and Shute Hill form the background.

A part of the old Railway Station, 1893. Two men are dismantling the roof to the right, ready for the new station completed the following year at the cost of £19,041. It seems that this original building dating from 1846 had become something of a joke in the town. Made from timber, it had been dubbed 'Noah's Ark'.

Both platforms show up well in this Edwardian study of the 1895 station. The footbridge, almost one hundred feet long, had small wooden tiles fitted to the treads which survive together with the platform benches, to the present day.

The Omnibus to Bishopsteignton in the 1890s. Above the horses is the bridge across the railway line giving access to Barnpark Road.

Mr Parker (left) was the only cab driver allowed into Station Yard until the 1860s. Horse power was used for heavy goods haulage until the 1950s.

Motor taxis in Station Yard in the 1930s. Cottages lining Myrtle Hill form the backdrop. A 1942 air raid caused damage to some of the properties in the terrace.

Lower Brook Street in the early 1970s. The sheds are back-to-back with Station Road and on the left, part of a corner terrace of brick built homes, one of which has a 'Sold by Lewis and Rowden' poster in the window. All the foreground buildings were demolished soon after this photograph was taken.

French Street, *c.* 1971. Experts believe that a farmhouse stood on this site in medieval times. Between the wars, allotments flourished here. A £1 million dual carriageway inflicted on the town during the late 1960s and early 70s sterilised all antiquities. Happily, Teignmouth Museum and Historical Society established itself in the tallest of these buildings and a dedicated membership of one hundred and fifty help to preserve and exhibit a wealth of fascinating artefacts and materials.

The second phase of dual carriageway construction is in progress in the early 1970s. Brook Hill School is about to be demolished. Turmoil on this site was repeated in 1997 when the westbound carriageway was ripped out to make way for the new supermarket.

High-sided concrete retaining walls were constructed (early 1970s) between the Railway Station platform and Myrtle Hill above. Next to the United Reformed Church stands Alberta Mansions used as the town's hospital from late in the nineteenth century until the provision of a new one on Mill Lane in 1925. The Mansions became apartments for permanent letting until the site was developed into a cluster of sheltered homes known as Alberta Court with its sister community (St Mary's Court) on the other side of Dawlish Road.

The bridge over the railway line at Shute Hill was originally bordered by a high stone wall which, together with the cottages, Drill Hall and school (left) was eradicated during re-development.

Beechcroft House occupied a large plot extending from Salisbury Terrace to Higher Brimley. At the time of this picture (1920s) it was occupied by the McLeods who also owned much of the neighbouring terrace properties. Early in the 1960s, the old house was demolished and a bright modern residential home for the elderly took its place. Following use only as a day care centre in the 1990s, Beechcroft is currently undergoing an extensive facelift and is due to re-open in 1998.

Midland Bank corner, Den Road, 1913. A shark with jaws wedged open for added interest is wheeled through town as a novelty to boost the annual street collection in aid of Teignmouth Hospital. Another twelve years passed before the new one was opened on Mill Lane.

Summer in 1939. Floods in Den Road have attracted a crowd of onlookers.

Orchard Gardens, possibly during the Great War. Uniformed men on horseback follow the flag-bearing float surrounded by Girl Guides and Boy Scouts. The letters could be B.P. for Baden Powell, (Founder of the Scouting Movement) perhaps? The handsome architecture can be appreciated from this high viewpoint.

Garden Place was tucked in behind Fore Street where St James flats now stand. Members of the Phillips, Cox and Broom families have decorated the courtyard in celebration of the coronation of King George VI and Queen Elizabeth in 1937. Distinctive light-coloured bricks have been laid as stepped paving.

Demolition in Fore Street in the 1960s. The combination of air raid damage and post-war development resulted in some 2,000 new homes being created in the town between 1946 and 1972.

Looking down Fore Street in the 1960s. None of these buildings exist now except for Five Ways Corner (right) with its characteristic arched windows. The popular Prince of Wales Inn is beside the temporary barricade at the junction of Fore Street and Higher Brook Street.

Five Ways in the 1930s.

The top end of Higher Brook Street, c. 1963. This terrace ran parallel to the southern boundary of the railway line between Fore Street and Shute Hill.

Somerset Place in the 1930s. A telegraph pole stands in the middle of the road just beyond the junction with what was then known as Gales Hill. The Lyceum, in company with the Riviera and the Carlton cinemas was enjoying a heyday. This part of town was reclaimed from marsh in the nineteenth century. The River Tame which divided Teignmouth before being under-grounded, once ran into the Teign near Rat Island next to Eastern Dock.

This magnificent Victorian complex of market, town hall, public baths, fire station and local board offices cost £6,400 to build in 1883. The official opening by the Earl of Devon incorporated a five gun salute, peels of church bells, bands and a grand procession.

The interior of the market in 1935. Commemorative mugs marking the Silver Jubilee of King George V and Queen Mary line the tables prepared for the tea party arranged for the town's children. Planks have been laid along the seats, presumably to assist the young ones to reach the tabletop.

Late in the afternoon of 13 August 1942, one of the worst of its twenty-one air raids left Teignmouth without a town hall, fire station and market. This was the scene in Northumberland Place after eight bombs killed fourteen and injured twenty-three and devastated property in Barnpark Terrace, Myrtle Hill, Higher Brimley and Parson Street.

Coysh's Olde Devon Dairy, Northumberland Place in the 1930s. The smart delivery van proclaims the fact that the dairy had been established for one hundred years, and a notice board (right) bears the legend 'Satisfaction comes from where our cream goes'. Out of business hours, jugs of scalded milk could be bought cheaply from the side door. The large letter 'A' (top right) is for Agra Engineering Works that operated in Devon Arms Yard.

Teign View Place Victory Tea Party in May 1945.

Regulars of The Blue Anchor wear festive buttonholes as they crush into the 'chara' for a trip out. A miniature anchor suspended from a rope is draped across the bonnet - a lucky emblem perhaps? A white-aproned matron, hands on ample hips, stands next to a bare-footed boy who straddles kerb and hub cap.

The Blue Anchor, Teign Street, c. 1897. The tenants, Mr and Mrs Riddler, are pictured with their granddaughter Mabel. A cat adorns the bar window and at the far side, a VR letterbox can be seen in the wall - and it's still there today! Gas lighting in the streets was replaced by electricity between the wars.

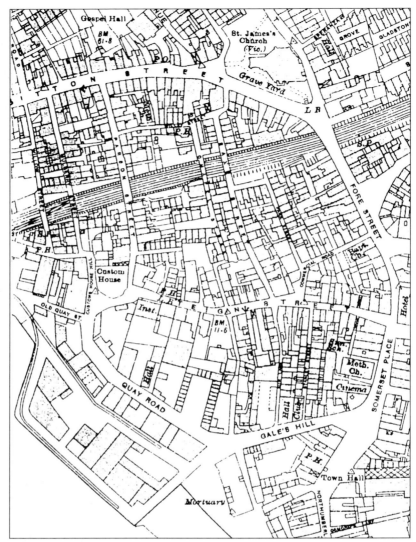

A map of 1935 shows a network of tiny streets clustering around the harbour. Street names that feature on the map include: Teign Street (originally Market Street) where, during the eighteenth century, weekly markets were held on the site of Shimell's Yard. Chapel Street gained its name from the primitive Methodist chapel situated there. A pound for stray animals was at the foot of Park Street. Parson Street, where the curate of St James resided. Willey Lane with its Soup Kitchen. Saxe Street, named after the Saxe-Coburg family, was probably the oldest street in town. Scown's Lane once called Donkey Lane because of the stables at the end close to the mouth of the River Tame where it met the Teign. Globe Lane, named after a tavern became Sun Lane, which in turn was named after the pub that stood on its Teign Street corner. Furze Lane was renamed after Stanley, the nineteenth century explorer. Bitton Street named for Bishop Bitton of Exeter who used Bitton Manor as a summer retreat in the fifteenth century. Commercial Road with its Royal Oak Inn. Mulberry Street (built almost four hundred years ago) that ran from Bitton to the Tame via Scown's Lane, long before the existence of Teign Street. For 'Old Teignmothians' these names will conjure up thoughts of the past when a closely-woven community inhabited this much altered part of town.

The Regia Hotel (re-named Harbour Lodge in the 1990s) stands at the junction of Teign and Parson Streets. This 1920s view shows a pergola stretching from the side entrance (right) to the western boundary with Old Quay Street.

Park Street Garage, known as 'Buckingham's' was replaced by Pellew Arcade in the 1960s. This is the junction of Commercial Road and Teign Street looking north towards the railway line just prior to development. A sign right of the shop door directs motorists to turn right for Newton Abbot, Exeter and Torquay.

The flats lining Bitton Park Road break the skyline and to the right, a derelict terrace awaits the same fate as the foreground, 1960s. The cottages on the left slope remain as the western side of Parson Street.

Gales Hill in 1912. Originally constructed as the Atheneum Theatre in the 1840s (which cost £1,000) it became a drill hall for the Devon Artillery before the Unionist Club moved in. In the 1960s when the Conservative Club were re-developing the interior, some one hundred year-old frescoes from its use as a theatre were discovered. They are still on the walls, but behind the panelling. The building went up for sale in 1997.

Jewellery, watches, spectacles, walking sticks and even umbrella making was on offer at Pedrick's in Fore Street, 1910.

Down in the 'lost streets' where the town's close-knit community had their roots, these little homes offered their occupants a much improved living standard than that endured by previous generations. Fortunately, the days of poor parishioners depending upon financial relief from the conscience-stricken wealthy for survival have advanced. When this area was cleared to make way for a dual carriageway, the residents scattered to other parts of town. Those with long memories need little prompting to recall their lives in these streets.

Looking down Parson Street, early 1960s. The former Seaman's Mission on Teign Street (Teignmouth House) towers over the rooftops.

An air raid on 10 January 1943 caused twenty deaths. Saxe Street pictured here during the clearing up, was hit by a bomb that passed through several houses, skidded in the roadway and bounced up before exploding. Six other bombs made their mark on Powderham, Alexandra and Salisbury Terraces as well as Bitton Street.

An alert at 12.47p.m. brought a four bomb raid killing five residents of Park Street. Numbers 7, 8, 12 and 13 were badly damaged and 14 to 16 had to be demolished.

Park Street in 1960. Pellew Barn at the lower end, standing out in white next to its drab neighbours is the only building to survive to the present day. The little Austin A30 is parked outside a timber framed hall erected in the 1950s for use as the Joyce Ridge Dancing School as well as a Red Cross Training Centre.

Commercial Road, c. 1962. The north wall of the Baptist church faces the Royal Oak public house. Every Friday between the wars, cattle ferried in by rail were driven down here to a slaughterhouse on the left. The children are approaching Park Street now Pellew Arcade.

Bitton Street, 1929. Locals gather outside Martin's boot and shoe stores to await a glimpse of HRH The Prince of Wales in the royal motor car during a short visit to the resort.

Bitton Street pictured in a post-raid clearing up. In the middle of the row (right) is a brick bomb shelter, it is along this stretch that the new Exeter Road, cut down through The Groves in the 1960s joined with Bitton Street.

The Gospel Hall (centre) suffered severe bomb damage as did St James church, the roof being set on fire by one of the twenty-one raids endured by Teignmouth.

Bitton Street in the early 1960s when it was the main thoroughfare. A lorry collecting empties from Cocking's Dairy and a clay lorry on its way to the docks cause congestion.

Gloucester Road. A trio of HE bombs caused the death of six people and injuries to sixteen on 2 July 1942. Groups of award-winning flats now stand here.

An overview from newly built Pellew flats in September 1967. Distinctive windows highlight Pellew Barn (right) adjacent to the junction of Park Street and Commercial Road. Five Ways corner stands out (left) and part of Orchard Gardens next to it.

Towards the end of the 1960s. Demolition work to make way for new homes and a dual carriageway has begun - Teignmouth is about to be sliced in half and her old heart gouged out.

Two
River Teign and Harbour

In this section we look at the estuary of the River Teign as it turns south with the tide and squeezes between The Point and Ness to join the English Channel.

The wooden bridge across the Teign completed in 1827 was considered to be the longest in England at 1,671 feet, *c.* 1900.

The manager of Teignmouth Gas Works occupied the house next to the mud-ridden and horse manure decorated lane that served as a main route to Newton Abbot early this century. Many improvements were made in the following years and in 1996/7 major re-construction of the stretch between Inverteign Drive and Salcombe Dip was undertaken.

Teignmouth and Shaldon
BRIDGE AND FERRY.
2 POUNDS
REWARD.

NOTICE is hereby given, that whoever will give Information of any Person or Persons who shall feloniously take or retain any of the Materials of the **BRIDGE**, or who shall wilfully injure any of the Property of the Bridge Company, shall on Conviction receive a Reward of *two Pounds*.

And all Persons having any of the Materials of the **BRIDGE** now in their Custody are requested forthwith to deliver over the same to the Bridge Keeper.

THE FERRY BOAT

Will ply from *Six o'Clock in the Morning, till Ten o'Clock at Night, until the 1st of October, and a commodious Boat is provided for conveying Horses and Carriages across the Ferry.*

JOHN CHAPPELL TOZER,
Clerk.

Dated, July 2nd 1838.

CROYDON, PRINTER, &c. TEIGNMOUTH.

Lord Clifford, who owned the ferry rights was paid £4,000 compensation when the bridge was opened in 1827. Tolls collected averaged about £950 per annum in the early years. The cost of £28,000 was met by the newly-formed company with shareholders subscribing to £25 shares. Timber piles, some eighteen inches square supported the twenty-three spans, the middle sections collapsing just seven years later due to an attack of worm. Copper was used to cover the replacement columns but a further collapse occurred in 1893.

A replacement bridge of stone was constructed in 1931. To the left of the gate is a list of tolls (now housed in Teignmouth Museum) which were applied until compulsory purchase by Devon County Council in 1948 at a figure of £90,000.

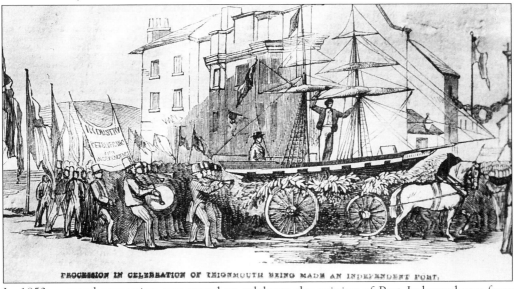

PROCESSION IN CELEBRATION OF TEIGNMOUTH BEING MADE AN INDEPENDENT PORT.

In 1853, a grand procession was staged to celebrate the gaining of Port Independence from Exeter. Led by a herald on a white horse, it featured sailors, rope and sail makers, harbour and river masters, fishermen, smiths, plasterers, builders and sawyers - every man carrying a tool of his trade. The banner 'Industry, Perseverance and Independence' demonstrates the anticipation of future wealth, an intention toasted at the dinner for three thousand rounding off the notable occasion.

Success of the harbour was slow. Facilities were gradually extended but it took a century to achieve the huge tonnage anticipated in 1853. The mooring of two, three and four masted schooners mid-river was a common sight up to the 1930s.

Coal Quay, 1930s. Colliers bringing in up to 900 tons of coal for the town's gas works and Newton Abbot's power station were invariably one of Everard's. London registered with mid-ship bridges, their names ended in 'ity'- such as *Serenity*. The siding just beyond the railings allowed coal trucks to be shunted (by The Elephant) on to the main line. Renwick, Wilton and Dobson's Coal Office was within the enclosure (left) where, in the 1920s the German cruiser *Stuttgart* was broken up. Its generators provided the town with electricity. Also on this site, concrete blocks were manufactured by Jack Phillips.

Coal Quay was on western dock, next to Polly Steps, shown here in the 1930s. A steam crane unloads coal from the ship's hold and drops it into the sifter. Screens separate it into different grades and three railway trucks are loaded simultaneously.

A six-ton sentinel steam lorry nose-dived off Eastern Quay in the 1930s. Built for Devon Trading Company at Bideford in 1933, it was known as 'The Lion' and undertook local deliveries of building materials until 1964. The driver, Harry Bartlett escaped injury.

No.1 Dock, 1930s. The *Suffolk Coast* with a white chevron on its black funnel belonged to Coastlines Shipping Company. The vessels drew about seventeen feet of water and could only enter the harbour once a fortnight on a spring tide. Rapid unloading of cargoes of oil cake and soap from Liverpool was essential to allow the vessel to depart on the next tide. *Gustav* occupies the other berth of No.1 Dock which is still in use today. No.2 Dock was filled in during the 1990s, to allow for longer ships.

No. 1 Dock in the 1950s. Clay was brought in from local quarries by rail and by road. These trucks will have been emptied by shovel but five ton lorries in the 1950s to twenty ton lorries in the 1980s had to reverse up 'big ramp', the triangular-topped structure between shed and ship. Some thirty yards long, it was constructed by Evan Evans and Bill Tribble, employees of Teignmouth Builders, Best and Son. Clay was tipped straight into the hold of the ship, speeding up the handling process.

Unloading slates from the continent in the 1950s. About one thousand tons a year were imported, each slate being individually handled into packs of ten. Dockers include, from right to left: Bill Hook, Mark Nason, Fred Hook and George Henry Boyne. Asbestos sheets piled behind were handled with no thought of health risk. If the sheets got wet, the men found that their hands became shiny and nicotine stains vanished as if by magic.

Coal Quay, 1970s. Within a decade, the power station at Newton Abbot was to close. These rails were ripped out and a traditional import spanning over a century ceased. None-the-less general import and export tonnage increased even though the coal trade had ended. In 1984, total tonnage was 720,000.

The Old Quay Inn stood between the railway line (note signal box) and No.2 Dock. The landlord organised coach trips in the post-war years. More than forty ladies line up for the camera before squeezing into the waiting vehicle.

Families gather to celebrate the Coronation of Queen Elizabeth II on 2 June 1953. Beneath the royal portrait is the legend 'Let's drink a health unto Her Majesty'. A lion and unicorn are partly obscured by the greenery flanking the portrait.

'The Elephant', a sentinel steam road tractor bought by the Quay Company in 1931. Fitted with large timber buffers, she was used to shunt rail wagons before being sold in 1963. After preservation she changed hands several times and is now in the Netherlands. Crown bottle caps were used to pick out the company name on the roof.

Outlook from New Quay in the 1950s. Mussel tanks were built into the quay in the foreground which, in 1967 was extended by a wooden pier for the landing of catch from local trawlers. Eastern Dock with 'big ramp' is to the rear, Devon Trading Company leasing many of the sheds for their trade in builders' merchants materials.

Many of the buildings recorded here in the early 1970s would disappear in the next few years. The Old Quay Inn and storage sheds gave way to large-scale transit sheds, changing the face of the harbour for all time. The western end first phase of the dual carriageway, Douglas House and Pellew Street blocks of flats are complete.

After nearly a century of use, sheds on the corner of Quay Road have become dilapidated, January 1981. It is time for demolition.

A wider view from Parson Street flats shows the scene a few days later with clearance under way. On the left-hand edge of the photograph is the old Seaman's Mission, Teignmouth House, on Teign Street.

New Quay Inn, *c.* 1900. Wrongly captioned The Old Quay, this shot confirms that sand levels were much lower at that time, the flight of steps in the right-hand corner shows up twice its current length. Sailing ships were berthed alongside the quay where repair works could be conveniently undertaken.

New Quay, *c.* 1900. The inn was established as 'The Newfoundland Fishery' in 1661 but changed its name when the new quay was constructed in 1820. Two men lounge close to the large metal mooring ring (still in use today) and a pale figurehead is just visible on the two mast schooner.

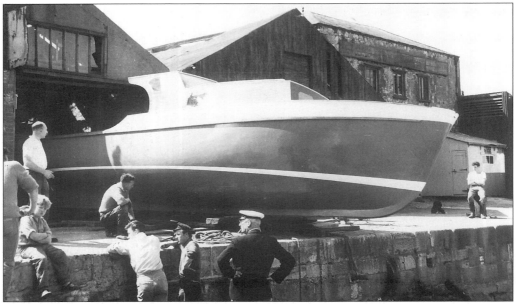

Syd Hook (second from the right) stands next to the New Quay whilst Stan Hook inspects the hull of the *Orinda*, the owner, Mr Chandler, looks on. The year is 1959. Hook Brothers set up as boat builders on the New Quay in 1946 and in the following forty years, with four employees, built one hundred and twenty vessels.

Construction of the *Goldeneye*, a thirty-five foot motor yacht by Hook Brothers 1952/3. Ketch-rigged with three hundred and ninety square feet of sail, she had a diesel engine. The hull was mahogany planked on an oak keel stem stern frame and timbers. The owner paid the wages, plus 3/6 per hour (18p) for launching and trials and £60 on completion, as well as £4 per week for overheads.

Teign View Place on the river beach in the 1950s. Not a patio in sight! Nets are draped on the mooring post (timbers from the original bridge to Shaldon) retained by the Harbour Commissioners for securing ships beached for bottom maintenance.

River beach in the late 1960s. A British film *Press for time* starring Norman Wisdom was shot in the town. One sequence involved a double-decked bus (minus windows on the upper deck) being driven down Ivy Lane and into the Teign.

The importance of dating photographs (not necessarily on the front) cannot be sufficiently emphasised. It becomes a reference point for numerous other pictures and allows the archivist opportunity to confirm features, or lack of them, by a specific date. To the left of New Quay, this wonderfully sharp image gives a glimpse of properties lining Teign Street before Eastern Dock was developed.

Gann and Palmer occupied Strand Shipyard early in the twentieth century but went to the wall when the Great War broke out. A sign at the end of the row of small huts states 'Motor boats. E.F. Hook' and next to the open sail, A. Pittaway's pleasure boat advertising board can be seen. The trees are within the garden of 'Riverside'- a substantial nineteenth century gentleman's dwelling demolished in 1986.

Morgan Giles Boat Yard occupied the river frontage between Forester's Terrace and Lifeboat Lane from the 1920s until its demise in 1968. The wartime workforce of one hundred and eighty concentrated on Admiralty demands for seventy-two foot motor launches, gun and torpedo boats; pinnaces and thirty-five foot harbour launches and repairs to damaged craft in the channel. When the US Navy base (servicing landing craft) was set up adjacent to the yard, secret work on submersible craft began. Marina Hotel on the end of Powderham Terrace was commandeered for training crews who later progressed to Slapton to rehearse for the Normandy landings on D-Day in 1944.

A post-war leisure boom saw Morgan Giles production turn to magnificent Monaco cruisers. Despite their appeal, these so-called 'floating gin palaces' failed to save the company from financial difficulties followed by closure. The corrugated boat shed, offices and patent slip disappeared, the site bought up for development and by 1990, a large complex of riverside flats named Morgan's Quay and Leander Court was established. It became possible to walk the entire length of the river beach for the first time in living memory when a boardwalk was constructed as part of the development.

The Strand in the late 1950s. A small Monaco motor boat has been loaded on an Eggbeer's lorry which will transport it to the London Boat Show. A group of Morgan Giles workforce are, from left to right: Alec Dodd, Reg Robbins, Roy Mills, Brian Gilpin, Rob Webster, Kevin Gill (known as Tonto) and George Briggs.

Ferries old and new, early in the twentieth century. A hand-rowed service across the mouth of the Teign began in the eleventh century with the fares passing to the Duke of Cornwall. The rights later belonged to The Cliffords as lords of the manor who sold them in the 1820s to the Bridge company.

The bottom of Lifeboat Lane in the 1950s. More than fifty people queue for a pleasure boat trip or the ferry to Shaldon. Note how open the surrounding hills appear compared with today.

The Arnold (1890s) outside the lifeboat station built in 1862 on land given by the Earl of Devon. Teignmouth was one of the first places in this country to receive a lifeboat from the Shipwrecked Fishermen and Mariner's Benevolent Society, superseded by the RNLI in 1854.

The Point from Torquay Road, 1903. The Harbour Commissioners blasted rocks from the foot of the Ness and employed a £300 mechanical blower to dislodge sand in order to improve access for shipping. In 1904, the existing three berths together with five new ones handled imports of 15,529 tons. Note how closely the river flows to the lifeboat station.

Three
Hinterland

Around Teignmouth's compact centre lies a half-circle of land cut by three approach roads, two with steep gradients. The western boundary smudges into rural landscape, remnants of which can still be enjoyed today despite extensive development on the hillsides.

Chelsea Place, 1929. Residents await the passing of the royal motor car carrying HRH The Prince of Wales.

A Tantivy stagecoach photographed on Dawlish Hill just above the Woodway junction, *c.* 1900. Two small children stand in the road, oblivious to potential danger.

The lower end of Dawlish Road, *c.* 1900. Nearest the camera (right) is the Catholic church of Our Lady and St Patrick and below is the Congregational church re-named United Reformed in 1972. St Michael's, the parish church of East Teignmouth overshadows the surrounding properties with its tower of 1887.

Dating from a time when the resort boasted numerous fine hotels for well-heeled visitors, Higher Woodway Hotel stood on the upper side of New Road. It was demolished in 1990 and developed by a Housing Association.

A souvenir postcard, produced for the pleasure and convenience of hotel visitors, shows the interior displaying a charm that now belongs to a past age.

AVENUE LEADING TO
Barnpark Pension, Teignmouth.

The deserted, tree-lined Barnpark Road of yesteryear bears no resemblance to the car-littered thoroughfare of today.

Woodlands Hotel, Barnpark Road sometime in the 1950s. Despite being tucked away, Woodlands has survived as a hotel to the present time. Occupied (late 1700s) by wealthy local banker, Mr Holland, legend has it that when the threat of invasion by Napolean was feared, he buried his treasure in the grounds and it has never been discovered.

Early in the twentieth century, Barnpark Terrace was the epitome of elegance and good taste. With four floors above ground and another 'below stairs', the properties were commodious and well suited to summer occupation by large Victorian families. Well kept parkland in the foreground set off the south side of the terrace to perfection.

On 13 August 1942, No.1 Barnpark Terrace was wiped out in an air raid. Fortunately for those people trapped in the wreckage, one of the air raid wardens had been a miner and he immediately sunk a five-foot shaft and tunnelled through to rescue them. This was the worst day of the war so far with eight bombs, fourteen deaths and almost fifty injuries. The rescue services were aided by personnel from the armed forces and a temporary respite centre was set up in West Lawn School.

A quiet afternoon on the lower end of
Ferndale Road, *c.* 1908

Higher Brimley Terrace, *c.* 1910. These sturdy Victorian homes were enhanced by terracotta features around the doorways and red and yellow brickwork in alternate layers in the bay windows.

'The Groves' comprised Avenue, Terrace and Crescent clustering on south facing slopes above the harbour. The Crescent pictured here with nonchalant boy posing by a gatepost is also seen in the background of the next shot.

The gentlefolk who once languished on the verandah of Landscore House (top right) could not have imagined how the demands of road users would dictate the future. The Exeter Road is being developed, in the 1960s, and was soon to be dubbed 'Death Hill' following serious traffic accidents.

Grove Avenue, 1910. The houses on the left have survived to the present day but those on the right were swept away by development of the Exeter Road.

The Kingsway prefabs stand out on the hillside to the left of Teignmouth Hospital, *c.* 1962. New flats line Bitton Park Road. Mount Everest and Yannon Towers are easily distinguished. The dual carriageway and Exeter Road have yet to be built and most telling of all, Coombe Valley is nothing more than fields and trees, lanes and hedgerows.

BITTON LODGE, TEIGNMOUTH.

Looking down Clay Lane, *c.* 1910. To the right is the east end of Bitton Avenue and on the left, trees mask a lodge known as Westcliff Cottage. It was thought to have been part of seventeenth century Teignmouth House (not to be confused with the Teign Street property with the same name) which was bought up in 1863 together with Westcliff House and Lower Bitton House by Mr John Parson, Chairman of the Metropolitan Railway. Lower Bitton House was demolished and Westcliff renamed Bitton House. The lodge was demolished after war damage and a telephone exchange built on the site.

Alexandra Terrace and Bitton Avenue above were developed by a local builder, Mr F. Slocombe, who purchased the Bitton Estate from Mr Parson in 1899.

Numbers 6 to 10 Alexandra Terrace were deleted from the council's valuation list on account of war damage caused on 10 January 1943. The town's worst raid brought five Focker Wolf 190s, dropping five HE bombs killing twenty and injuring twenty-eight others. One hundred and eighty-three homes were damaged and twenty-one were later demolished.

On 2 March 1941, the town's sixth air raid claimed a family of three and a middle aged couple in their homes on Second Avenue. Up until that dreadful night, only one other resident had fallen victim to enemy attack despite eighteen months of conflict.

Mill Lane, *c.* 1930. The lane got its name from Bitton Mill, long since demolished. Large circular grinding stones from the mill can be seen in the west wall of Third Avenue just beyond the junction with Mill Lane.

Kingsway, June 1946. Councillor E.W. Parsons, Chairman of Teignmouth Urban District Council officially opens the first prefabricated home. The provision of inexpensive and readily available housing was essential to a town that lost two hundred and twenty-eight homes and a further 2,250 damaged during twenty-one air raids of the Second World War. The prefabs were warm and served their occupants well until replacement by houses and flats some years later.

Coombe Farm at the beginning of the twentieth century. In recent years, the upper floor has been brought into use and gable windows added in the thatch.

On the lower side of the farmhouse, to the right was a red brick building which can still be seen today.

Four
Everyday Life

The next section is all about people and how the daily round encompassed going to work, attending school, worshipping at church, enjoying some leisure time. Although the details have changed beyond recognition, the underlying pattern of everyday life continues to revolve around those fundamentals.

A delivery wagon pauses outside Farleigh House at the turn of the century.

A group photograph believed to be Teignmouth Police Force, *c.* 1907.

Teignmouth Laundry, Station Road, 1914. Seated second from the right is Henrietta Paddon whose family owned the Ship Inn. She married Sidney Briggs in 1918 and within seven years, he was to become a local hero. Together with Commander Martin (Founder of the Royal Ocean Yacht Club) the first Fastnet Race, six hundred miles of tough British waters, was won by Sidney in the *Jolie Brise*, a French pilot cutter. The Laundry continued to serve the town for many more decades. A 1930s advert promises 'You will experience a sense of pleasure in finding it return home like new'.

Deep excavations outside Venice House on the Esplanade show drainage pipes about eight feet below the road surface. The man in front seems to be standing in a brick-lined inspection pit.

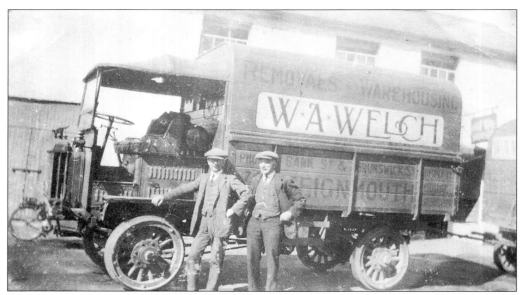

Welch's removal van in the 1920s. Bill Coleridge(left) was one of the town's earliest motor drivers, working also as a chauffeur. Welch's had premises in Bank Street and Brunswick Street and a store on the quay.

The post office staff pictured in Den Road in the 1930s. The telephone exchange was situated here and later removed to Clay Lane. The workforce of around forty-five is similar to present day numbers.

Jack Clampitt mowing the Den Bowling Green late in the 1930s. He was the youngest head gardener ever appointed by the Urban District Council. Note the canvas covered lorries parked at Den Crescent.

Laying turf for the Den Bowling Green in 1909. It cost 2d to play for an hour during its first season. The council workmen to the left wear knee pads.

Teignmouth Fire Crew in 1956. Pickford's depot on the quay was severely fire damaged and whilst two crew members continue the fight against the flames from a high ladder in the background, their colleagues succumb to the pleasures of a WVS mobile canteen menu.

The Fire Station at First Avenue in the 1950s. Declared the best-kept station in Devon on more than one occasion, the new HQ was provided following temporary use of County Garage after the main fire station in Northumberland Place was destroyed by enemy action in 1942.

Fire at Ye Olde Gift Shoppe, Teign Street, 16 October 1951. Sun Lane entrance is to the right of Sims the furnishers occupying No.39. This property has been the base for the *Teignmouth News* since the 1980s.

Teignmouth Rugby Club during the 1953/4 season. Orest Tosio, Club Secretary for over thirty years, is seated on the right of the front row. The Talbot Inn in the background was demolished to make way for County Garage car sales lot in the 1990s.

Teignmouth Cricket Club, c. 1950. Pencilled on the back of the original picture are the names Bosanquet, Brock, Braunton, Matthews, Bonner, Hampson, Wills, Laing, Cornwall-Brooks (headmaster of Lendrick School and captain of the team) Baulkwill, Blaydon and Curtis. Before the war, the club had to play at Oaklands, Dawlish.

Maypole Stores, Bank Street in the 1950s. Margaret (Renfree) Wood (left) recalls that butter had to be 'knocked up' into blocks from bulk. Rationing was still on so butter allowance was two ounces per person per week. Dried fruit arrived in waxed paper lined wood crates. Clusters were broken up, then weighed out into bags in the back store. Despite the labour intensive work-style, it had to be service with a smile! Margaret entered the grocery trade when she was fifteen and stayed for forty-four years.

Staff of the Pier shop in 1951. Roma Davies, Lil Brown, Dyllis Quantick, Alice Northcott, Phyl Satchel and Bertha Herbert pause for the camera. In the window, a miniature maestro invites passers-by to visit the Pier Ballroom.

Lendon the butcher, Fore Street, c. 1910. Sides of beef, pork and lamb hang open to the elements, long before exhaust fumes filled the streets and the word 'pollution' entered everyday parlance. Before demolition (in the 1960s) the shop was run by Stanley Rowe who served as TUDC Chairman in 1957/58.

Reginald Blackmore (left) outside his shop in Hollands Road with the delivery boy, Dennis Rice and greengrocer Hudson from across the road. The feathered Christmas fare of the mid-1930s was invariably plucked by the purchaser. In later years, this became a convenient sweet shop for Brook Hill School around the corner.

The hunt outside the Royal Hotel in 1963. Possibly the Dart Vale and Haldon Harriers sporting jackets of dark green.

Noel Nathan in the 1920s. 'Nunk' to his many friends, was a jockey. Pictured in Pomeroy's stables in Mere Lane, Noel became an artist in later years spending the final ten years of his life working on a huge collection of West Country harbour scenes that now enhance the corridors of Torbay Hospital.

Fish Quay in the 1930s. Newly constructed underground sewage tanks provided a spacious area for fishermen to mend their nets. The old name for these parts was Rat Island because it was cut off at high tide. The River Tame joined the Teign here and the Ferry Boat Inn was built on rising ground in its estuary early in the sixteenth century. When religious persecution caused Catholics to hold services in secret, the inn was used, sometimes the priest hiding in the spacious chimney. It was re-named the Jolly Sailor after the ferry service was moved further down river.

Salmon fishing up-river, c. 1900. Seine nets have been in use since biblical times. Whilst the hauling-in is underway, a river barge slips past on a gentle breeze.

New Quay beach in the 1930s. No smiles at such a poor catch! Young George Henry Boyne (see also page 53) on the left is next to George Highgate, Jack Boyne and Dickie Boyne.

Ernie Chapman, *c.* 1950. Whelk pots consisting of a metal frame encircled with rope and baited with crab were set in the river during neap tides. Whelks caught out in the bay were tougher than those harvested in the Teign. Born in 1910, Ernie caught lobsters and prawns and worked mussel beds from the age of eighteen. For over sixty years the local waters provided him with a living and it was only after becoming an octogenarian that he finally hung up the salmon seine nets.

Fred Niblett, New Quay Beach, 1936. Fred was Teignmouth's last gas lamp lighter. The year after this photograph was taken, a newly formed electric company was illuminating the town's streets in a brighter manner. To the rear, Ship's View and Bridge View, the latter having been converted from a store in 1934. It became the author's home in 1994.

Station Road in 1939. A wooden packing case is pressed into service as a boat and two young lads wearing the cheekiest of grins pose for the camera as they loll against the motorvan. The butcher boy at Wills has propped his bike in the usual place and pauses to be included.

Teignmouth Follies, c. 1930. Started up by Ada Winstanley and Norah Parker in the late 1920s, the girls helped charitable causes by providing entertainment with song and dance routines. A second wave of Follies continued after the war but the group disbanded in 1963. Joyce (Winstanley) East wears the plain dress and Nell (Gait) Tibbs is on the left at the end of the row. A reunion held in 1996 attracted sixty former Follies who could still recall the various routines learned in their youth.

Living chess, the Den, c. 1930. Pupils of Brook Hill School kept visitors amused by enacting chess games after weeks of tuition by their teacher, Mr Egginton who, together with another instructor sat on step ladders calling out the moves. The 'pieces' are distinguished by their headgear.

Barbara Spencer Edwards established a Dancing School in Teignmouth during the 1950s. Numberous pupils including Sir John Gilpin benefitted from her previous experience as a professional dancer. Pictured early in the 1960s, 'Bras', as she was affectionately known was a stickler for discipline. After her death in 1990, a memorial tablet was set up in the foyer of the Carlton Theatre by Joan Lambert who continued to run the school into the mid-1990s.

The Gay 90s Old Tyme Dance Club in the 1950s. Weekly dances were held in the ballroom of the London Hotel (see initials on the pelmet) and membership numbered around one hundred including the Mills, Mortimore, Hitchcock and Turpin families. Rita Menghini sits in the centre.

Coombe Vale Road, December 1964. Captain Michael Morgan-Giles (Chairman of the TUDC) lays the first brick of Quinnell House on Yelland's nursery land, bought up for the purpose three years earlier. The Bishop of Crediton blessed the completed complex of thirty-four flatlets for elderly people almost two years later.

Bitton Park Road, c. 1971. Mary Collins and her brother Roy pictured on the bench set up in memory of their parents, Mr and Mrs Marks Collins who ran a bakery on the site from 1920 to 1969. The property was demolished.

Teignmouth Warships Week, November 1941. Mr Irish, (centre) Chairman of the TUDC, is flanked by visiting members of the Armed Forces. Councillors stand at the rear of the bandstand that faced inland across the Den. The aim was to raise £160,000 for a Corvette.

Bitton House, April 1949. Shortages of everyday commodities persisted long after the war. A dry cleaners lorry was pressed into service by Teignmouth Rotary Club to distribute canned goods to the over seventies, sent from fellow Rotarians in Queensland.

The Chairman of TUDC, Frederick Davidson and the Town Clerk, Mr Theodore Lee Edwards at Bitton House, 1948. An appeal for Christmas tree toys was launched within the community to help brighten the festive season during the post-war time of shortages. Mary Collins is third from the left.

Coronation Tea Party at the top of Kingsway, June 1953.

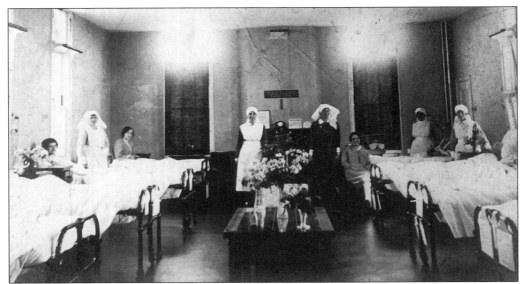

In 1925, a new hospital (costing £17,000) was opened on Mill Lane by Lady Cable of Shute Hill House where, during the First World War, wounded servicemen were nursed. The new facility had an operating theatre, x-ray equipment, four private wards and two general ten-bedded wards. On average each year, patients numbered around one hundred in and seven hundred out.

Teignmouth Hospital after a ten bomb raid of 8 May 1941. The assault began at 2.15a.m. The fire brigade, first aid and rescue parties, together with extra helpers from Dawlish rushed to the scene to evacuate casualties. The death toll was eleven, including three nurses. Hermosa Lodge became emergency premises until the replacement opened in 1954. It was the first general hospital to be built in Britain after the introduction of the NHS in 1948.

Members and officials of TUDC, September 1945. Chairman, Henry Irish OBE served throughout the six years of conflict. The most significant item on the council's agenda was the re-construction of a severely damaged town. The plans were prepared by an eminent architect, Professor Adshead. A copy of his work may be studied in the reference section of Teignmouth Library.

Sidney Silverston was the much-revered headmaster of Teignmouth Grammar School from its inception in 1920 until his retirement in 1954. His approach to pupils was based on the commitment to achieving the 'greatest happiness for the greatest number'. In a school magazine interview he observed 'children do not change much but now they allow too much to be done for them. Cinema, wireless, cheap literature is readily available, they do not exert themselves sufficiently'. He was a councillor for the Urban District, a Rotarian, and a member of the once flourishing Debating Society.

St Michael's Church, c. 1870. A man takes his ease on the inset bench whilst three more pose with two small boys who moved during the plate exposure and consequently appear as faint spectres. Note the fine detail of the gateposts but the tower of 1827 looks shabby. It was replaced by the handsome limestone version in 1887, commemorating the Golden Jubilee of Queen Victoria.

The combined choirs of St James and St Michael's Church in the late 1930s. Ken Boobyer (third from left in the front row) went on to achieve acclaim in the world of bowls.

Dedication of Christchurch, Kingsdown Road in the early 1950s. Bishop Willis of Uganda performed the ceremony. Less than half a century later, lack of congregation caused the little place of worship to be sold and developed into a private house.

The Sunday school children of the Congregational Church during the turn of the century. Following major upheavals caused by the opening out of the tunnels between the railway station and Eastcliff in the 1880s, this new church was built on Dawlish Street.

The Menghini family outside their refreshment hut on the beach opposite St Michael's Church, c. 1935. The family made their own ice cream for sale and supplied tea trays at 4d (2p) per person. Young Ernest who later became Harbourmaster for the port and his sister Carmen remember when high seas and poor weather necessitated the removal of the hut and all its contents to the prom' until later in the day when it had to be re-instated on the sands.

Summer visitors in Coombe Vale in the 1920s. The junction with Deer Park is close to the houses in the background. Bungalows were soon to be built on the right bank.

Junior Theatricals in Coombe Vale, 1930. Albert Best kept a horse (just visible on the right) in his field where the performers pose for the camera prior to touring a play to outlying towns and villages. Employees of Best's hardware business in Somerset Place made scenery and props and everyone helped out in those happiest of times as recalled by Margaret (nee Full) Whitlock in the centre of the back row. George Young, a ship's chandler had the bungalows built.

The convent of Notre Dame (now Trinity School) viewed from the air in the 1930s. Buckeridge Towers, used as a dormitory is in the left-hand corner. Diagonally opposite, glass houses and perfectly ordered fruit and vegetable plots flourish. The convent was originally a monastery constructed (from 1826) on Bugridge farm land by the Redemptorist Order of Priests and Brothers. The congregation of the public church of Notre Dame purchased the buildings and established a boarding school for girls in 1901.

Corpus Christie Day at the convent in the 1920s.

Carnival procession in Fore Street when crowds of enthusiastic onlookers lined every yard of the route to smile, wave and throw copper pennies onto their favourite floats, in 1960. The annual event was summer's highlight, the town's population almost doubling for the week. Everyone involved in the holiday trade could depend upon a good boost to income and worked together for the shared goal of success. Those times are held in great affection, as is Neta Drew pictured with her son and daughter on the float 'Pink for a girl, blue for a boy'. Known to two generations of youngsters from both sides of the estuary, Neta's dancing classes continue to be as popular as ever today. Invariably amongst the winners, her family's floats were always eye-catching. Note the thousands of paper roses. After participating in twenty-nine annual processions, Neta bowed out in 1974. No-one has replaced her, Neta Drew was, unquestionably, this town's carnival sweetheart!

Five
Favoured Resort

Record-breaking sunshine hours and unspoilt charm made Teignmouth a south coast favourite.

An overview of the Den and seafront, c.1920.

The Singers' Pavilion straddling the sea wall provided informal open-air entertainment up to the early 1930s when it was destroyed by a high tide. The town's coat of arms adorns the top of the proscenium arch with the legend 'Bohemian Concert Party'-Chas. Sedbury Proprietor. Al fresco performances did not please everyone, the council employed an inspector of nuisances to investigate any problems that might damage the reputation of this much-admired resort. Note the position of this pavilion between pier and lighthouse on page 103.

In about 1900, even earlier than the previous photograph a timber 'concert hall' occupied the same spot although the barrel-supported structure was down on the sands.

On East Beach, just beyond the pier, a piano and two sheets of board are all the trio of entertainers had to work with. The refreshment hut and a row of bathing machines stretch towards the esplanade.

Bathing machines have been supplanted by neat tents and there are two long shelters beside the sea wall, c. 1920. Mole's pleasure roundabout stood beside the slipway next to the pier which was greatly extended after severe damage in 1908. No Den Pavilion, no car parks in front of Den Crescent or Courtenay Terrace - in fact, no cars!

Teignmouth Pier, designed by Joseph Wilson of the Crystal Palace School of Engineering dates from 1865. Four pavilions and an ornamental ironwork bridge form the entrance. These may be the earliest photographic studies in existence. The difficulty of carrying heavy equipment was more than compensated for by the pin-sharp images obtained.

Midway down the pier looking back to the seafront. Apart from the pavilions at the entrance and rows of seats running the full length, there are no other features, suggesting that the photograph is one of the first ever taken. A series of arches bearing globular lamps, the same as the one seen at the entrance, was added later. The original function of the pier was to provide access to large pleasure steamers.

Gas globe-bearing arches are faintly visible and a concert hall has been added to the sea-ward end, *c.* 1925. Trippers queue on the landing stage for the arrival of the paddle steamer *Duchess of Devonshire.*

Numerous children crowd the barrier whilst a horse show is in progress on the Den. Steps lead to an upper deck on the pier and a trio of boys have cheekily climbed up beyond the others.

Mid-pier in the 1930s. The original seating remains and a quartet of cottage-style shops have been added.

During the Second World War, the pier was partly severed to deter enemy use as a landing stage. Windbreaks had been added by the 1950s.

Overview in the 1930s. A large ballroom for dances and shows has been added. The four little shops are seen between the entrance and the mid-pier hall and a further two in the same style on the next open stretch. The Den Pavilion and enquiry bureau are visible as is St James church.

The *Sea Belle* was one of at least eight local pleasure boats that hovered on the front beach in those long-gone days when the resort was packed out all through the season.

Teignmouth Swimming and Lifesaving Society organized waterpolo matches adjacent to the pier early in the twentieth century. Spectators crowd the local workboats to catch a close view of the players, some of whom became Devon County Champions.

In the world of swimming there was no greater champion than Harry Smith who frequently swam from the pier to Babbacombe or from Parson and Clerk Rocks then up the Teign to Hackney. A small boy sporting the TSLS badge overtly expresses his pride in being pictured with a local hero.

Innocent pleasures found from sand and sea brought visitors back to the resort year after year. Whilst segregated bathing was enforced, East Beach was for female use. The child on the bathing machine steps is looking over her shoulder. Camera shy perhaps, or has she spotted the man lurking behind the next machine?

Edwardian seaside amusement. Punch and Judy execute a traditional routine for the young at heart. A hand-cart plies 'pure ices' and a boy in a long apron (right) is selling items from a tray.

Edwardian ladies shunned the sun with parasol or large hat. The contented looking group have settled on West Beach, the gentlemens' side for bathing. Presumably, ladies were able to sit where they wished during the segregated bathing regime.

What would the seaside have been without open-air gatherings to praise the Lord? In common with other resorts, Teignmouth attracted multitudes of children on Sunday school outings by rail or charabanc who were drawn into 'al fresco' style worship on the sands. On the right, a lady accompanies the hymns with a portable organ.

The Local Board acquired the Den from Lord Courtenay in 1869. Deep sand dunes were supplanted by a level grassed area allowing activities of all kinds. Bicycles, including Penny Farthings, were raced, as were donkeys. More unusual were the pig races (nearly every backyard had one) staged for visitors' amusement. The Royal Hotel with its original roof line together with Powderham Terrace make a graceful backdrop.

Powderham Terrace, 1943. A five bomb air raid on 10 January knocked out three buildings to the left of Lynton House Hotel. A Sound Location Unit was employed to find survivors beneath the rubble. Several years later, the properties were expertly rebuilt, the new blending perfectly with the original.

The occasion is unknown but probably dating from the lead-up to the First World War. Uniformed men standing shoulder to shoulder form a barricade on the Den. A band and choir are the centre of attention for the photograph taken from the balcony of the Royal Hotel.

This picture almost certainly ties up with one showing crowds outside the pier (page 107) gathered for an event on the Den. It may be a carnival for at the rear to the left of the gas lamp, a tableau banner reads 'Under the spreading chestnut tree'. The smallest of the fancy dress pony riders looks less than happy !

Teignmouth Regatta has been an annual event since late eighteenth century. For many years, Hancock's Fun Fair was a centrepiece and crowd-puller. Steam driven roundabouts, barrel organs and the helter skelter offered fun for the less affluent.

West Beach and Royal Hotel in the 1920s. Bathing machines, beach tents and Punch and Judy were essential components of the perfect seaside holiday. Easy access by rail and motor cars becoming commonplace meant more visitors and Teignmouth rode the crest of the popularity wave between the wars.

The Royal Hotel in the 1930s. Occupying pride of place on the Den and enjoying over a century of success, this elegant hotel fell victim to declining tourist trade in the 1970s. It was purchased for re-development into retirement flats. Local people fought to retain the building for tourism but after almost a decade, during which time the Royal Hotel became an eyesore, permission was granted and work commenced in 1997.

The Royal Hotel's ballroom, c. 1962. The town's most favoured venue for notable functions was used for concerts, banquets, balls, meetings and parties. On this occasion, members of Teignmouth Operatic Society, founded in 1900, have gathered around the bandstand for a spot of music-making.

Whalebones by the lighthouse in the 1920s. Many pieces of bone, including the jawbones to form an arch, were placed on the Den. Two similar arches were erected at Eastcliff. The curiosities were donated to Teignmouth by a founder Director of Teignmouth Quay Company, Mr Pike Ward.

SUNKEN GARDENS, TEIGNMOUTH   52

Promenade sunken gardens in 1950. Storm damage in 1989 resulted in this feature being filled in to form a raised flower bed.

In the late 1930s, a yachting pool was created on the promenade. To mark the official opening, local boatman 'Pixie' Matthews built a replica of Drake's *Golden Hind* generating much delight for onlookers.

In 1994, a former town mayor, David Tickell, located the five foot long replica which had been missing for many years. Len Matthews (left), son of 'Pixie', marvels at the sails made by his mother nearly sixty years earlier.

The Peter Pan Railway with three engines was a great post-war favourite until wheels of a different kind (bikes and rollerboots) took over the pleasant prom'.

The Den Bowling Green, *c.* 1919. Spectators had the use of benches sheltered by the bank between rinks and prom'. Folding canopies provided shade over the benches, note right-hand corner. Close-by, a pair of tree trunk sections have been up-ended for use as summer planters.

Den Pavilion which opened in June 1930. Constructed of iron and glass, it cost £3,500. Front stalls numbered 190, mid-auditorium had 238 seats, behind those, a further 457. The lighting provision amounted to £130 worth of equipment. Within its first year of operation, the licensee was making financial losses, setting a trend that was to continue for some years. In 1984, Teignbridge District Council leased it to the Teignmouth Players. Threat of demolition has hung over the building since the publication of a local plan late in the 1980s. It has survived to the present time.

A transformation scene. Dressing rooms were added as part of extensive refurbishment - the Den Pavilion became the Carlton Theatre in 1967.

The Public Assembly Rooms (right) were erected in 1826 as a memorial to Admiral Pellew's victory (1816) at the Battle of Algiers. Lord Courtenay and forty shareholders raised the capital cost of £2,000. East Devon and Teignmouth Club bought it in 1890, stayed eighteen years and sold it to Charles Sayce who converted it into the Riviera Hotel. Moving pictures were shown in the first floor ballroom in 1912 by Charlie Poole. Bill and Katie Prince paid £2,500 for it in 1924, continuing the dual use of cinema and hotel. In 1934, it became a 900 seat super cinema costing £33,000. Declining trade caused the stalls to be separated for use as an amusement arcade in 1970, film and stage shows continuing to attract audiences to the first floor to the present day.

Riviera Cinema in the 1950s. *Moulin Rouge* was showing during carnival week so an octet of suitably attired young ladies took part in the procession before being photographed on the cinema's balcony for publicity purposes. The conservatory has been removed and the balcony open to the elements as was originally intended.

The Den and new enquiry bureau, *c.* 1939.

Compare this trio of pictures spanning almost a century. Taken from the pier built in 1865, the first shows St Michael's church with the old tower. It was replaced in 1887, dating the photograph to within a twenty-two year period. A sandy bank separates beach from promenade and the Esplanade is dominated by a five storey pair of hotels, The Berkeley and The Esplanade.

A 1920s summer season is in full swing. A new sea wall protects the promenade from winter storms and St Michael's tower stands sentinel over East Beach.

The last great wave of seaside holidaymakers captured on film before cheap flights to foreign parts tempted tourists away, probably August Bank Holiday in the mid-1950s. The void caused by the loss of the hotels on the Esplanade in 1942 was never filled despite proposals to create a circular concert hall and theatre on the site outlined in a post-war town plan.

Here is a close-up of the duo of fine hotels that were demolished after being seriously damaged by an air raid on 2 September 1942. The Berkeley (left) and The Esplanade.

Channel View and Devon House marked the end of Courtenay Terrace at its junction with Esplanade. Built in the early nineteenth century by Courtenay, lord of the manor of East Teignmouth, the family coat of arms was incorporated in the wall just above the pair of gateposts and can still be seen.

Den House and Bella Vista in the 1920s. Small features worth noting are the ice cream seller in a white overall (centre), the perambulator, and small girl (right) on the slope looking wistfully towards the sands.

Clifton House, *c.* 1910. Apartments for the summer offered here were the earliest self-catering holidays. Mere Lane emerges (right) at the seafront next to the handsome terrace known as Spring Gardens.

Spring Gardens, c. 1925. This building was named after Eastcliff at one time and in the 1960s it earned an enviable reputation as the Bairnscroft Hotel, specializing in accommodating families. The raised walkway in the background was often referred to as Old Maid's Walk, note the pair of arches made from whale jawbones at either end.

Whalebone arch, c. 1925. Mr Pike Ward, a prominent townsman was deeply interested in artefacts from Iceland where he traded for fish in the years around the turn of the nineteenth century. He donated the bones and others (see also page 117) to the town in 1924. This pair was removed to allow the emplacement of a large gun early in the Second World War. The pair closest to town remained in place for several more years until they were found to be rotting and removed to an allotment near the railway line at Broadmeadow.

Mordref, c. 1920. East Devon and Teignmouth Club moved here from the Riviera. Card and billiard rooms were available for the membership of over one hundred. The property was demolished and replaced by the Lido swimming pool in 1962.

Overcliff in the 1940s. The weekly tariff for full board in one of the twenty-five rooms was five guineas in 1950. The building was demolished and the site cleared in the 1960s to become a car and coach park taking its name from this property as it was known before the war, Eastcliff. The parapets of Slocombe's railway bridge are in the foreground.

The child's joyful expression embodies the spirit of Teignmouth's golden years between the wars. Those happy times when everyone knew one another and were pleased to share their beloved hometown with holiday visitors. More significantly, it was managed by people who dwelt within its boundaries and who were able to make decisions that were sympathetic to the unique character of Teignmouth.